The Bread Machine Cookbook
Special Abridged Edition

Donna Rathmell German

BRISTOL PUBLISHING ENTERPRISES, INC.
San Leandro, California

a nitty gritty® cookbook

Cover design: Frank J. Paredes
Cover photography: John A. Benson

Printed in the United States of America.

ISBN 1-55867-227-3
Part# 60275

Special abridged edition of
The Bread Machine Cookbook
has been produced for
Salton•Maxim Housewares, Inc.

CONTENTS

INTRODUCTION

Shortly after purchasing an automated bread machine in 1989, I became frustrated by the lack of bread machine recipes. When other owners were queried, although excited about the machines, nearly everyone was dissatisfied with the available recipes.

When this book was first published in 1991, there were no other cookbooks available for bread machines nor were there any manufacturer "help" lines available for individuals to turn to. People turned to me for answers to their bread machine baking questions or to share their hints and ideas. The *Hints and Trouble Shooting* chapter is the direct result of many of these contacts.

I urge you to read the information in the chapters that precede the recipes themselves. Many of your questions will be answered before you begin baking bread, and many problems that you may have had will be avoided by reading these chapters. The techniques you learn in these pages will help you to produce a perfect loaf every time.

Join the millions of bread machine owners who are finding delight and satisfaction in producing an endless variety of delicious loaves in their own kitchens!

ABOUT BREAD MACHINES

Before beginning, it is important for you to become familiar with the owner's manual and/or the recipe book that came with your machine. *To use these recipes in your machine, add them to the baking pan exactly in the order listed.*

In general, a 2-pound machine can use up to 4 cups of bread flour, although I find that 3½ cups usually results in a nice loaf of bread at or just over the lip of the pan. A total of 4 or 5 cups of combination flours (bread flour mixed with whole wheat, oats, rye, corn, etc.) can easily be used and up to 6 cups of whole grain flours. It is necessary to keep an eye on the dough to prevent overflows. For a full 2 lb. machine, use the Large recipe.

Unlike any other bread machine cookbook on the market, I give you three different sizes for each recipe. If you don't want to make such a large loaf of bread, choose a smaller formula.

If at any time it sounds like the machine is struggling with a large amount of flour, add a tablespoon or two of water (or more if necessary) to soften the dough. If the machine is struggling, it could cause damage to the motor.

The sides of the machine may require scraping to help get all ingredients to the kneading paddle. Use a rubber spatula, never a metal one, for scraping. Once the dough has formed a ball it will do just fine and can be left alone. If it has taken the machine a long time to knead the ingredients into a ball, you can stop the machine and start the cycle from the beginning, giving the dough a little longer time to knead.

One of the main concerns about using too much flour is that it could flow over the sides of the pan. Usually, you will just end up with a mushroom — the dough may cook onto the lid of the pan, or may not cook properly at the top. The real mess, however, is when the dough spills down the sides of the pan into the inside of the machine and onto the heating elements. Cleanup is a messy, time-consuming chore (I've done it often in testing). It is difficult to remove all dough from the heating elements, but it burns off the next time the machine is used.

It is wise to check the dough during the second rising period. If it looks too high, use a bamboo skewer (or something similar) and pierce deep into the dough to deflate it. Do not use metal objects, which could scratch the pan. In the worst case scenario, remove a portion of the dough. This enables you to at least salvage something!

BREAD INGREDIENTS

YEAST

A living plant, yeast eats sugar and produces carbon dioxide, which mixes with the gluten in flour to make the dough rise. Simply stated, without yeast your bread will be flat. Both active dry and fast-acting yeasts can be purchased either in envelopes (1 envelope equals about 2¼ tsp.) or in vacuum-packed jars.

In recent testing, fast-acting yeast (sometimes called rapid rise or quick yeast) consistently resulted in loaves that rose higher than those made with regular active dry yeast. Compressed (cake) yeast is not recommended for use in bread machines.

Yeast responds to ambient temperatures. It may be necessary to increase the amount of yeast in colder weather or to decrease it in very hot temperatures. However, too much yeast can cause air pockets or air bubbles.

LIQUIDS

Liquid ingredients should be warmed to lukewarm for the best performance. The liquid should be warm or comfortable to the inside of your wrist — baby bottle temperature, or about 110°.

Some ingredients that are used for liquid (fruits, vegetables, cottage cheese) may initially be difficult to knead into the dough. It is helpful to scrape down the sides of the pan with a rubber spatula and push the ingredients toward the kneading paddle. Once the paddle has picked up all ingredients, let it knead by itself for about 5 minutes; then, check the dough's consistency again for a smooth dough ball. If the process has taken quite a long time, you may wish to turn off the machine and start it from the beginning. This gives the dough a longer kneading period once it has achieved the correct consistency.

Because the moisture must be pulled out of fruits (banana) or vegetables (potato or spinach) it may require a longer period of kneading before a judgment can be made as to whether to add more liquid. If lumps of the fruit, cheese or vegetable are still visible, chances are that you should let it knead longer before you add water. If you add water too early, you may end up with dough that is too moist. Should this happen, add flour, 1 tablespoon at a time, until a smooth ball of dough forms. Always use very ripe bananas for the best moisture content.

FATS

In bread baking, fats provide flavor, moisture and a soft texture. Fats used interchangeably include margarine, butter, vegetable oils, shortening or lard. Some recipes specify olive oil, as it imparts a distinctive taste; however, you can use any vegetable-based oil. Unlike conventional bread baking, butter or margarine need not be melted before being placed in the machine. Applesauce or apple and orange juice concentrates (found frozen in cans) can be substituted tablespoon for tablespoon for fats.

SWEETENERS

A necessity in yeast bread baking, sugar and sugar substitutes feed the yeast, enabling it to rise. In addition, they assist in the browning of the crust. Sugar substitutes for bread baking include brown sugar, honey, molasses, maple syrup, and even jam, jellies or marmalades. Honey is also a natural preservative for your breads.

SALT

A growth-inhibitor of the yeast, salt provides a counterbalance for the sugar. It also brings out the flavor of the bread. If breads are not rising, try cutting the amount of salt.

EGGS

A nonessential ingredient, eggs are sometimes used in bread baking to add richness, color and flavor. Egg substitutes were used for testing when fractions of eggs are called for. If you prefer not to use the fractions of eggs, you can omit the egg and adjust the consistency of the dough with milk or water as needed.

One egg yolk or white can be substituted for ½ egg. One large egg equals about ¼ cup of liquid. Egg substitutes are based on this amount also. One half an egg equals approximately ⅛ cup or 2 tablespoons of liquid.

FLOUR

There are many different kinds of flours, grains or cereals that can be used for structure in bread baking. As a general rule, white or bread flour should be at least 50 percent of the flour or grain used. A higher percentage will result in a heavy, dense, low-rising bread. With that "rule" in mind, flours can be substituted cup for cup with other flours, grains or cereals. A detailed description of various grains and flours follows.

While making yeast breads, you normally use a wheat flour base which, when kneaded, develops *gluten*. Gluten is an elastic substance that traps the carbon dioxide released from the yeast. Gluten is the key ingredient in the wheat that makes the dough rise. Nonwheat flours, which contain less gluten, must be mixed with wheat flour to a maximum ratio of 1 to 1. The higher the amount of non- or low-gluten flour, the smaller and denser in texture your bread will be.

The most common flour for bread baking is that obtained from wheat. One walk down the flour aisle of your local grocery store will tell you that there are several different kinds of wheat flours. Differences are due to where the wheat is grown (making it hard or soft), what section of the wheat kernel is used, or how the flour is milled and what treatments are provided after the milling.

All-Purpose Flour: A blend of hard and soft wheat flours that can be used for a variety of baking needs, including breads and cakes. All-purpose flour loses many of its natural vitamins and nutrients during the milling process. Hence, it is usually "enriched" by replacing four of those nutrients: iron, thiamine, riboflavin and niacin. Bleached all-purpose flour is chemically whitened; unbleached flour is allowed to whiten naturally.

Bread Flour: This is the recommended flour for most of the recipes in this book. Bread flour is derived from hard wheat, meaning it is high in both protein and gluten. You will find that bread flour will give you a finer grain bread than bread made from all-purpose flour. You may also hear this flour referred to as "bromated," a process which adds a dough conditioner to enhance the gluten's development. If your grocery store does not carry bread flour, do not hesitate to ask the management to add it to their inventory.

Whole Wheat Flour: Milled from the entire wheat kernel, this is light brown in color and contains all of wheat's natural nutrients. A healthy addition to bread, whole wheat flour is lower in gluten than white flour. Breads made with whole wheat flour will not rise as much as those made from bread flour. You may also see a version of whole wheat flour referred to as graham flour.

Vital Gluten (Gluten Flour): The gluten protein is removed from wheat flour by rinsing off the starch. This starch is then dried and ground to be added to regular white bread flour. Pure gluten is slightly gray in color, but does not affect the color of your bread. It can be purchased through a well-stocked health food store or by mail order sources. Vital gluten can be added in small amounts to your dry ingredients in low-gluten bread dough to achieve a lighter texture.

CORN

Cornmeal: Ground from corn kernels, cornmeal is found in any grocery store. Yellow cornmeal is the most common variety, but also try white cornmeal, which is milled from white corn, and blue cornmeal, milled from blue corn. Corn is less nutritious by itself than many of its grain cousins.

OATS

Rolled Oats: The grinding of oats leaves the bran and germ and, therefore, the nutrients intact. Fairly high in protein, oats are also high in vitamins B and E. Rolled oats are the most familiar form of oats to most of us. The grains are steamed, rolled into flakes and dried.

Oat Flour: This is simply milled or ground rolled oats. Make your own in your food processor or blender: blend oats, 1 cup at a time, at high speed for about 1 minute, until a fine flour forms. Look for it at health food stores or by mail order.

RYE

Rye Flour: Milled from the rye berry or the entire rye kernel, rye flour has a high nutrient content. The darker the color, the stronger the taste and the nutrient value. There is no gluten in rye flour; it must be used in combination with a white wheat flour in bread baking. The larger the percentage of rye in the bread, the smaller and denser the loaf will be.

BUCKWHEAT

This grain is very high in protein. It can be found in flour form in many grocery and health food stores. Nutritionally, buckwheat is rich in vitamins B and E and is high in calcium.

HINTS AND TROUBLE SHOOTING

Before beginning, I strongly recommend reading two things:

1. The owner's manual that comes with your machine.
2. The introductory chapters of this book.

Don't be afraid of the new machine. It really is as simple as 1-2-3-4-5:

1. Measure the ingredients and put them into the pan exactly in the order specified.
2. Choose the desired cycle and crust setting.
3. Press the start button.
4. Check the dough after about 5 minutes of kneading to ensure that the dough has formed a round, smooth ball. If not, adjust the dough's consistency with flour or liquids (see page 12).
5. Remove the fully baked loaf of bread from the machine at the completion of the baking cycle.

Perhaps the single most important thing to check is the consistency of the dough after 5 to 10 minutes of kneading.

Don't be afraid to open the machine briefly during the kneading process. Open it long enough to check the dough's consistency and then to make any adjustments necessary. Don't leave the lid open for long and don't open it during baking.

DOUGH CONSISTENCY

When making bread, whether by hand (the old fashioned way) or by machine, the flour and other ingredients will pick up the moisture from the air. The moisture content of the grains themselves may vary, as will the absorbency of whole grain flours, according to how they were milled. As a result, on any given day the dough may have too much liquid, which could result in an overflow or a sunken top.

When kneading dough by hand, you develop an ability to *feel* the right consistency. When kneading dough by machine, you can *see* the right consistency. Let the machine knead the dough for about 5 minutes and then look at the dough. With few exceptions, it should form a nice, smooth ball. Sometimes the ball will be round, and other times it may take on a cylindrical shape that "tornadoes" up the side of the pan.

By watching the dough on a regular basis, you will soon develop a sense for what looks right. If you stick your finger in and touch it, it should feel moist, but not really be sticky. Dough that is too dry will not mix properly or it may cause the machine to struggle (you'll hear it). Or, the dough may be uneven (not smooth) or form two or more balls of dough instead of one. If this is the case, add more liquid, one tablespoon at a time, until the desired dough consistency is obtained. Conversely, dough that is too wet will not be able to form a ball. In this case, add more flour 1 tablespoon at a time until the desired consistency is obtained.

If you hear the paddle rotating, but the ingredients on top of the dough are not moving —

Check to see that the paddle is inserted properly. Sometimes the paddle was not placed on the kneading shaft correctly or it has slipped. The easiest way to check is to turn off the machine, reach in and feel whether the paddle is on correctly. It can usually just be pushed onto the shaft, and then the machine can be restarted without any difficulties (except for a messy hand!).

If the bread rises well but then collapses during baking —

In hot weather, the dough may be rising too fast. To prevent this, cut the yeast and sugar, increase the salt and/or use a shorter rising cycle. If hot weather is not the culprit, try using a smaller size recipe.

If the bread has a sunken top or a mushroom —

There is too much moisture in the dough. Cut back the amount of liquid by ¼ cup and add it in slowly as the machine is kneading. Stop adding it when the dough forms a smooth round ball.

If the crust is too dark or brown —

Bake the bread on the regular crust setting rather than the dark crust setting. If this is not the problem, try stopping the bread about 5 minutes prior to the end of the baking cycle. You can also cut the amount of sugar, which darkens the crust.

If the bread is not rising and/or is not baking properly (doughy) —

Use the Fruit & Nut cycle. Natural sugars found in fruits may actually inhibit the rising of bread and cause the bread to bake improperly. Or, cut down on fruits and other sugary substances. Too much butter or fat can cause a similar problem.

If the bread has large air bubbles —

Cut the amount of yeast used.

If the bread seems too heavy and dense —

Some breads may be heavy and dense just because of the ingredients. Nonwheat flours or meals, such as rye, oat or corn, do not contain as much gluten as wheat and will naturally be lower rising and denser than wheat. In addition, ingredients such as wheat germ or bran actually break the gluten strands, causing breads to rise less. When using large amounts of such grains, it may be helpful to add 1½ to 2 tbs. of vital gluten to achieve a higher rise and/or a better texture. Other reasons for breads not rising include a large amount of salt, which inhibits rising, and/or not enough sugar or water.

If raisins or similar ingredients do not mix into the dough evenly —

Any dried fruit can be lightly floured to prevent pieces from sticking to each other. You can also add these ingredients at the beginning of the second kneading cycle instead of waiting for the beep.

WHITE BREAD

This very rich bread is terrific for sandwiches. You'll find yourself going back for more and more. It is not, however, one of the more dietetic breads, but it's well worth the calories anyway! Use an egg white, egg yolk or 2 tbs. egg substitute for ½ egg.

	Small	**Medium**	**Large**
water	½ cup	¾ cup	1 cup
margarine or butter	2 tbs.	2½ tbs.	3 tbs.
egg	½	1	1
sugar	1½ tbs.	2 tbs.	2 tbs.
salt	¾ tsp.	1 tsp.	1½ tsp.
bread flour	2 cups	3 cups	3½ cups
nonfat dry milk	2½ tbs.	¼ cup	⅓ cup
yeast	1 tsp.	1½ tsp.	2 tsp.

SALLY LUNN

This very rich, European-style bread is loaded with butter and eggs and is not dietetic by any means! Set the machine for a light crust. The eggs give it lots of terrific taste and color. Tradition says that a young Englishwoman, Sally Lunn, sold this bread on the streets of Bath. Most bread cookbooks contain a version of this, which attests to its wonderful flavor. This is one of those breads that will never last to see leftovers.

	Small	**Medium**	**Large**
milk	½ cup	⅔ cup	¾ cup
margarine or butter	3 tbs.	¼ cup	¼ cup
eggs	1	2	2
salt	1 tsp.	1½ tsp.	2 tsp.
sugar	2½ tbs.	¼ cup	⅓ cup
bread flour	2 cups	3 cups	3½ cups
yeast	1 tsp.	1½ tsp.	2 tsp.

PORTUGUESE SWEET BREAD

Maria and Manuel, from Portugal, are living here while Manuel completes his doctoral degree. She has experimented with recipes to closely resemble those of her home country. This is one of my favorites.

	Small	Medium	Large
milk	½ cup	¾ cup	⅞ cup
eggs	1	1	2
margarine or butter	1 tbs.	1½ tbs.	2 tbs.
sugar	3 tbs.	¼ cup	⅓ cup
salt	½ tsp.	¾ tsp.	1 tsp.
bread flour	2 cups	2½ cups	3 cups
yeast	1 tsp.	1½ tsp.	2 tsp.

PORTUGUESE WHITE BREAD

A very light-colored, airy bread. It's slightly difficult to cut while hot, but who can wait until it cools?

	Small	**Medium**	**Large**
water	¾ cup	1 cup	1¼ cups
margarine or butter	2 tbs.	3 tbs.	¼ cup
sugar	2 tsp.	1 tbs.	1 tbs.
salt	¾ tsp.	1 tsp.	1½ tsp.
bread flour	2 cups	3 cups	3½ cups
yeast	1 tsp.	1½ tsp.	2 tsp.

ENGLISH MUFFIN BREAD

This is a really good, easy way to get that English muffin taste and texture. It's a great bread to set on the timer for a hot breakfast bread. In order to have the proper texture, there may be a sunken top to this bread.

	Small	Medium	Large
water	⅞ cup	1¼ cups	1½ cups
sugar	1½ tsp.	2 tsp.	1 tbs.
salt	¾ tsp.	1 tsp.	1 tsp.
baking soda	⅛ tsp.	¼ tsp.	½ tsp.
bread flour	2 cups	3 cups	3½ cups
nonfat dry milk	2 tbs.	3 tbs.	¼ cup
yeast	1 tsp.	1½ tsp.	2 tsp.

PEASANT BREAD

*This recipe is based on one given to me by Carmen, a friend and neighbor. It's a very moist, chewy bread with a light, crispy crust. It's absolutely wonderful with butter or cheese. It is somewhat similar to **English Muffin Bread**, but more moist. The dough will appear wet.*

	Small	Medium	Large
water	⅞ cup	1⅓ cups	1½ cups
sugar	1½ tsp.	2 tsp.	1 tbs.
salt	¾ tsp.	1 tsp.	1 tsp.
bread flour	2 cups	3 cups	3½ cups
yeast	1½ tsp.	2 tsp.	2½ tsp.

SOUR CREAM BREAD

This is a great sandwich bread with a nice texture and great taste. Warm the sour cream. Adjust the consistency of the dough with water as necessary (see page 12) and scrape the sides of the pan with a rubber spatula if you need to. As with any recipe with dairy products, do not make this on the timer.

	Small	**Medium**	**Large**
water	2 tbs.	2½ tbs.	3 tbs.
sour cream	1 cup	1⅓ cups	1¾ cups
salt	½ tsp.	¾ tsp.	1 tsp.
baking soda	⅛ tsp.	¼ tsp.	½ tsp.
sugar	1 tbs.	1½ tbs.	2 tbs.
bread flour	2½ cups	3⅓ cups	4 cups
yeast	1½ tsp.	2 tsp.	2 tsp.

CRUSTY CUBAN BREAD

This ethnic bread is very similar to a French or Italian Bread. It tends to be low-rising due to the lack of oil and small amount of sugar. Keep an eye on the dough and add a tablespoon or two of water if the dough looks dry or if the machine sounds like it is struggling (see page 12).

	Small	**Medium**	**Large**
water	¾ cup	1¼ cups	1½ cups
sugar	1 tsp.	1½ tsp.	2 tsp.
salt	¾ tsp.	1 tsp.	1 tsp.
bread flour	2 cups	3 cups	3½ cups
yeast	1½ tsp.	2 tsp.	2½ tsp.

FRENCH HONEY BREAD

This wonderful, slightly sweet French bread is lightly colored with a light, crispy crust. Expect a high-rising loaf.

	Small	**Medium**	**Large**
water	¾ cup	1⅛ cups	1¼ cups
honey	2 tsp.	1 tbs.	1½ tbs.
olive oil	2 tsp.	1 tbs.	1½ tbs.
salt	½ tsp.	¾ tsp.	1 tsp.
sugar	¾ tsp.	1 tsp.	1½ tsp.
bread flour	2 cups	3 cups	3½ cups
yeast	1½ tsp.	2 tsp.	2½ tsp.

ITALIAN BREAD

The recipe for this light-colored bread has been revised to give it a better rise, but it has less ethnic flavor than the original one. Add a tablespoon or two of water if the dough appears dry, or if the machine sounds like it is struggling (see page 12).

	Small	**Medium**	**Large**
water	⅞ cup	1¼ cups	1½ cups
sugar	1 tsp.	1½ tsp.	2 tsp.
salt	¼ tsp.	½ tsp.	¾ tsp.
bread flour	2 cups	3 cups	3½ cups
yeast	1½ tsp.	2 tsp.	2½ tsp.

BUTTERMILK BREAD

You can get great taste and texture and a light, fluffy bread without fresh buttermilk. Look for powdered buttermilk in the baking aisle of the supermarket.

	Small	**Medium**	**Large**
water	⅔ cup	1 cup	1¼ cups
margarine or butter	1 tbs.	2 tbs.	2 tbs.
sugar	1 tsp.	1½ tsp.	2 tsp.
salt	½ tsp.	¾ tsp.	1 tsp.
bread flour	2 cups	3 cups	3½ cups
buttermilk powder	3 tbs.	¼ cup	⅓ cup
yeast	1½ tsp.	2 tsp.	2½ tsp.

COTTAGE CHEESE BREAD

This rich, high-rising sandwich bread is a favorite of my husband. Warm the cottage cheese. Use an egg white or yolk or 2 tbs. egg substitute for ½ egg.

	Small	**Medium**	**Large**
water	3-4 tbs.	3-4 tbs.	¼-⅓ cup
cottage cheese	⅔ cup	¾ cup	1 cup
margarine or butter	1½ tbs.	1½ tbs.	2 tbs.
egg	½	1	1
sugar	2 tsp.	1 tbs.	1 tbs.
baking soda	⅛ tsp.	¼ tsp.	¼ tsp.
salt	¾ tsp.	1 tsp.	1 tsp.
bread flour	2 cups	2½ cups	3 cups
yeast	1½ tsp.	2 tsp.	2 tsp.

RICOTTA BREAD

This was a huge hit with friends and tasters who ranked it one of the best. It slices very well. Use an egg white, yolk or 2 tbs. egg substitute for ½ egg. Warm the cheese for a high rise, but puncture the dough during the second rising period if it rises too high (see page 3).

	Small	**Medium**	**Large**
milk	¼ cup	⅓ cup	½ cup
ricotta cheese	1 cup	1⅓ cups	1½ cups
margarine or butter	2 tbs.	2½ tbs.	3 tbs.
egg	½	1	1
sugar	2½ tbs.	¼ cup	⅓ cup
salt	1 tsp.	1 tsp.	1½ tsp.
bread flour	2 cups	3 cups	3½ cups
yeast	1 tsp.	1½ tsp.	2 tsp.

CREAM CHEESE BREAD

This delicious loaf is like a dessert bread or cake. Bring the cream cheese to room temperature or warm it in the microwave before using. Scrape the sides of the pan if necessary and adjust the dough's consistency with milk or water if you need to (see page 12).

	Small	**Medium**	**Large**
milk	1/3 cup	1/3 cup	1/2 cup
cream cheese	4 oz.	6 oz.	8 oz.
margarine or butter	2 tbs.	2½ tbs.	3 tbs.
egg	½	1	1
sugar	2 tbs.	3 tbs.	3 tbs.
salt	¾ tsp.	1 tsp.	1½ tsp.
bread flour	2 cups	3 cups	3½ cups
yeast	1 tsp.	1½ tsp.	2 tsp.

CHEDDAR CHEESE BREAD

Use grated or shredded cheddar cheese and lightly pack it into the measuring cup. The cheese may affect the consistency of the dough, so keep an eye on it and adjust the moisture if you need to (see page 12).

	Small	**Medium**	**Large**
water or milk	⅔ cup	1 cup	1¼ cups
margarine or butter	1 tbs.	1 tbs.	1½ tbs.
cheddar cheese, grated or shredded	½ cup	⅔ cup	¾ cup
sugar	2 tsp.	1 tbs.	1½ tbs.
salt	½ tsp.	¾ tsp.	1 tsp.
bread flour	2 cups	3 cups	3½ cups
yeast	1 tsp.	1½ tsp.	2 tsp.

WHOLE WHEAT I

This is my favorite whole wheat. It's a high-rising bread that slices very well.

	Small	Medium	Large
water	½ cup	¾ cup	1¼ cups
margarine or butter	2 tbs.	3 tbs.	¼ cup
egg	1	1	1
sugar	1½ tbs.	2 tbs.	2½ tbs.
salt	¾ tsp.	1 tsp.	1½ tsp.
bread flour	1½ cups	2 cups	2⅔ cups
whole wheat flour	¾ cup	1 cup	1⅓ cups
yeast	1 tsp.	1½ tsp.	2 tsp.

WHOLE WHEAT II

A subtle, different whole wheat. The yogurt gives it a great flavor and dense texture. I have always enjoyed oats with whole wheat. Warm the yogurt and use the water to adjust the consistency of the dough (see page 12).

	Small	**Medium**	**Large**
plain nonfat yogurt	1 cup	1¼ cups	1½ cups
water	¼ cup	⅓ cup	⅓ cup
margarine or butter	2 tbs.	2½ tbs.	3 tbs.
sugar	2 tbs.	2½ tbs.	3 tbs.
salt	1 tsp.	1 tsp.	1½ tsp.
bread flour	1½ cups	2 cups	2½ cups
oats	½ cup	⅔ cup	¾ cup
whole wheat flour	1 cup	1⅓ cups	1½ cups
yeast	1½ tsp.	2 tsp.	2½ tsp.

BRAN BREAD

This wonderfully hearty bread is so healthy! Wheat bran is also known as millers' bran and, like oat bran, can be found in health food stores. Yes, the salt is the same amount for all sizes!

	Small	Medium	Large
water	1 cup	1⅓ cups	1½ cups
margarine or butter	2 tbs.	2½ tbs.	3 tbs.
brown sugar	1 tbs.	1½ tbs.	2 tbs.
salt	1 tsp.	1 tsp.	1 tsp.
wheat germ	¼ cup	⅓ cup	½ cup
whole wheat flour	½ cup	⅔ cup	¾ cup
oat or wheat bran	1 cup	1⅓ cups	1½ cups
bread flour	1½ cups	2 cups	2½ cups
vital gluten, optional	1½ tsp.	2 tsp.	1 tbs.
yeast	1½ tsp.	2 tsp.	2½ tsp.

NINE-GRAIN BREAD

Whole Wheat or Basic cycle

Nine-grain cereal consists of cracked wheat, barley, corn, millet, oats, triticale, brown rice, soya and flax seeds. It is available for purchase either in bulk or boxed. Look for it in a large grocery store or natural food store. Seven-grain cereal can be substituted.

	Small	**Medium**	**Large**
water	1 cup	1⅓ cups	1½ cups
margarine or butter	2 tbs.	2½ tbs.	3 tbs.
brown sugar	1½ tbs.	2 tbs.	2½ tbs.
salt	1 tsp.	1 tsp.	1 tsp.
9-grain cereal	1 cup	1⅓ cups	1½ cups
bread flour	2 cups	2⅔ cups	3 cups
yeast	1 tsp.	1½ tsp.	2 tsp.

MULTI-GRAIN BREAD

This hearty, somewhat dense, full-of-fiber bread is wonderful with a home-made stew or soup. You can substitute cracked wheat for bulgur, if desired. Scrape the sides of the pan with a rubber spatula if necessary.

	Small	Medium	Large
water	1⅛ cups	1⅓ cups	1½ cups
vegetable oil	1½ tbs.	2 tbs.	2½ tbs.
honey	2 tbs.	2½ tbs.	3 tbs.
salt	¾ tsp.	1 tsp.	1½ tsp.
bulgur wheat	¼ cup	⅓ cup	½ cup
wheat germ	2 tbs.	3 tbs.	¼ cup
wheat or oat bran	½ cup	⅔ cup	¾ cup
rye flour	½ cup	⅔ cup	¾ cup
oats	¼ cup	⅓ cup	½ cup
bread flour	1½ cups	2¼ cups	2½ cups
vital gluten	1½ tbs.	2 tbs.	2 tbs.
yeast	1½ tsp.	2 tsp.	2½ tsp.

WHEAT GERM SESAME BREAD

This high-rising, light and airy bread is absolutely wonderful. Use an egg yolk or white, or 2 tbs. egg substitute, for ½ egg. Keep an eye on the dough during the second rise and puncture it if necessary (see page 3). If in doubt, make a smaller size. For variety, substitute anise or fennel seeds for sesame seeds.

	Small	**Medium**	**Large**
water	⅔ cup	1 cup	1¼ cups
vegetable oil	2 tbs.	2½ tbs.	3 tbs.
honey	2 tbs.	2½ tbs.	3 tbs.
egg	½	1	1
salt	½ tsp.	¾ tsp.	1 tsp.
wheat germ	2 tbs.	3 tbs.	¼ cup
sesame seeds	1 tbs.	1½ tbs.	2 tbs.
whole wheat flour	¾ cup	1 cup	1¼ cups
bread flour	1½ cups	2 cups	2½ cups
yeast	1 tsp.	1½ tsp.	2 tsp.

OATMEAL SESAME BREAD

Whole Wheat or Basic cycle

This delicious sweet bread is good choice for breakfast.

	Small	**Medium**	**Large**
water	¾ cup	1 cup	1⅓ cups
margarine or butter	1 tbs.	1½ tbs.	2 tbs.
brown sugar	1 tbs.	1½ tbs.	2 tbs.
cinnamon, optional	½ tsp.	¾ tsp.	1 tsp.
salt	½ tsp.	¾ tsp.	1 tsp.
sesame seeds	3 tbs.	¼ cup	⅓ cup
oats	⅓ cup	½ cup	⅔ cup
whole wheat flour	⅓ cup	½ cup	⅔ cup
bread flour	1½ cups	2 cups	2⅔ cups
yeast	1 tsp.	1½ tsp.	2½ tsp.

OATMEAL BREAD

Here's a terrific oatmeal loaf! Regular dry milk can be substituted for butter-milk powder.

	Small	**Medium**	**Large**
water	¾ cup	⅞ cup	1⅓ cups
margarine or butter	2 tbs.	2½ tbs.	3 tbs.
sugar	1½ tbs.	2 tbs.	3 tbs.
salt	½ tsp.	¾ tsp.	1 tsp.
oats	⅔ cup	1 cup	1⅓ cups
bread flour	1½ cups	2 cups	3 cups
buttermilk powder	3 tbs.	¼ cup	⅓ cup
yeast	1½ tsp.	2 tsp.	2½ tsp.

VARIATION: CINNAMON OATMEAL BREAD

This wonderful, sweet oatmeal bread is great for breakfast.

Add to recipe:

cinnamon	⅓ tsp.	½ tsp.	⅔ tsp.

HONEY NUT OATMEAL BREAD

While many grocery stores carry a honey nut oatmeal bread for sandwiches, this seems more of a dessert-type bread to me. It's absolutely delicious and is a must-try! If you're not using the Fruit & Nut cycle, add the nuts 5 minutes before the end of the second kneading cycle.

	Small	Medium	Large
water	⅔ cup	1 cup	1⅓ cups
vegetable or walnut oil	1 tbs.	2 tbs.	3 tbs.
honey	1 tbs.	2 tbs.	3 tbs.
salt	½ tsp.	1 tsp.	1 tsp.
oats	⅔ cup	1 cup	1⅓ cups
whole wheat flour	⅓ cup	½ cup	⅔ cup
bread flour	1 cup	1½ cups	2 cups
yeast	1 tsp.	1½ tsp.	2½ tsp.
At beep add:			
chopped walnuts	⅓ cup	½ cup	⅔ cup

SHREDDED WHEAT BREAD

This is a very tasty, different bread. If you have another favorite cereal, try it in place of the Shredded Wheat. It's a great way to use up the end of the cereal box! Grind the Shredded Wheat cereal in a food processor until finely crumbled. Or, put it in a locking plastic storage bag and crush it with a rolling pin. Adjust the moisture of the dough if necessary (see page 12).

	Small	**Medium**	**Large**
water	¾ cup	1 cup	1⅛ cups
vegetable oil	2 tbs.	3 tbs.	3 tbs.
honey	1 tbs.	1½ tbs.	2 tbs.
salt	½ tsp.	¾ tsp.	1 tsp.
Shredded Wheat cereal, finely crumbled	½ cup	⅔ cup	¾ cup
bread flour	2¼ cups	3 cups	3½ cups
nonfat dry milk	¼ cup	⅓ cup	⅓ cup
yeast	1 tsp.	1½ tsp.	2 tsp.

GRAPE NUTS BREAD

It is not necessary to soak the Grape Nuts for this bread, but add them 5 minutes before the end of the second kneading cycle or at the beep. The dough may seem a little soft until the nuts are added. Any of your other favorite cereals can be substituted for Grape Nuts.

	Small	**Medium**	**Large**
water	1 cup	1⅓ cups	1½ cups
vegetable oil	2 tbs.	2½ tbs.	3 tbs.
sugar	1 tbs.	1¼ tbs.	1½ tbs.
salt	¾ tsp.	1 tsp.	1 tsp.
bread flour	2 cups	3 cups	3½ cups
yeast	1½ tsp.	2 tsp.	2 tsp.
At beep add:			
Grape Nuts cereal	½ cup	⅔ cup	¾ cup

NEW YORK RYE BREAD

This is a low-rising, very dense, flavorful loaf just like you buy on the streets of New York. If you want a lighter, fluffier loaf, add the vital gluten, which is available at health food stores. The caraway seeds can be adjusted to taste.

	Small	Medium	Large
water	⅞ cup	1⅛ cups	1⅓ cups
vegetable oil	1 tbs.	1⅓ tbs.	1½ tbs.
honey	1½ tbs.	2 tbs.	2½ tbs.
salt	¾ tsp.	1 tsp.	1 tsp.
caraway seeds	2 tsp.	1 tbs.	1 tbs.
rye flour	1 cup	1⅓ cups	1½ cups
bread flour	1¾ cups	2¼ cups	2⅔ cups
vital gluten, optional	2 tsp.	1 tbs.	1½ tbs.
nonfat dry milk	3 tbs.	¼ cup	⅓ cup
yeast	1½ tsp.	2½ tsp.	1 tbs.

NORWEGIAN RYE BREAD

This is my favorite rye. There is a large amount of flour in this recipe. If the dough seems dry or the machine sounds like it is struggling, add 1 to 2 tbs. water (see page 12).

	Small	**Medium**	**Large**
water	¾ cup	1 cup	1¼ cups
molasses	⅓ cup	⅓ cup	½ cup
margarine or butter	2 tbs.	2½ tbs.	3 tbs.
salt	¼ tsp.	½ tsp.	¾ tsp.
caraway seeds	2 tsp.	1 tbs.	1½ tbs.
whole wheat flour	¼ cup	⅓ cup	½ cup
rye flour	1¼ cups	1⅔ cups	2½ cups
bread flour	1¼ cups	1⅔ cups	2½ cups
yeast	1½ tsp.	2 tsp.	2½ tsp.

LIGHT PUMPERNICKEL

This wonderful, light pumpernickel makes great sandwiches.

	Small	Medium	Large
water	⅔ cup	1 cup	1⅓ cups
vegetable oil	1½ tbs.	2 tbs.	3 tbs.
molasses	1½ tbs.	2 tbs.	3 tbs.
sugar	2 tsp.	1 tbs.	1½ tbs.
salt	½ tsp.	¾ tsp.	1 tsp.
caraway seeds	1½ tsp.	2 tsp.	1 tbs.
unsweetened cocoa	1⅓ tbs.	2 tbs.	2½ tbs.
rye flour	1 cup	1½ cups	2 cups
bread flour	1 cup	1½ cups	2 cups
vital gluten, optional	2 tsp.	1 tbs.	1½ tbs.
yeast	1 tsp.	1½ tsp.	2½ tsp.

DARK PUMPERNICKEL

This heavy, dense bread is terrific with soup and/or salad.

	Small	**Medium**	**Large**
water	1 cup	1¼ cups	1½ cups
vegetable oil	2 tbs.	2½ tbs.	3 tbs.
molasses	3 tbs.	¼ cup	⅓ cup
unsweetened cocoa	1½ tbs.	2 tbs.	2½ tbs.
brown sugar	1 tbs.	1½ tbs.	2 tbs.
instant coffee granules	1 tsp.	1½ tsp.	2 tsp.
salt	¾ tsp.	1 tsp.	1½ tsp.
caraway seeds	2 tsp.	1 tbs.	1 tbs.
rye flour	¾ cup	1 cup	1¼ cups
whole wheat flour	¾ cup	1 cup	1¼ cups
bread flour	1½ cups	2 cups	2½ cups
yeast	1½ tsp.	2 tsp.	2½ tsp.

RUSSIAN BLACK BREAD

Eat this wonderful, hearty bread with soup and/or salad or serve it as an appetizer with a crab dip! You can substitute dark molasses for barley malt syrup.

	Small	**Medium**	**Large**
water	1 cup	1⅓ cups	1⅓-1½ cups
vegetable oil	2 tbs.	3 tbs.	¼ cup
barley malt syrup	1 tbs.	1½ tbs.	2 tbs.
white vinegar	1 tbs.	1½ tbs.	2 tbs.
sugar	¾ tsp.	1 tsp.	1½ tsp.
salt	¾ tsp.	1 tsp.	1 tsp.
unsweetened cocoa	1½ tbs.	2 tbs.	2½ tbs.
minced dried onion	½ tsp.	½ tsp.	¾ tsp.
instant coffee granules	¾ tsp.	1 tsp.	1 tsp.
caraway seeds	2 tsp.	1 tbs.	1½ tbs.
fennel seeds	½ tsp.	½ tsp.	¾ tsp.
bread flour	2 cups	2½ cups	3 cups
rye flour	1 cup	1¼ cups	1½ cups
yeast	1½ tsp.	2 tsp.	2½ tsp.

CORNMEAL BREAD

This is wonderful with a Southern- or Mexican-style meal — if it makes it to the table. If you can find it in your health food store, try blue cornmeal. What a tasty, different treat! My bread testers thought at first that I was kidding, but asked for more after trying it.

	Small	**Medium**	**Large**
water	¾ cup	1 cup	1⅓ cups
vegetable oil	1 tbs.	1½ tbs.	2 tbs.
egg	1	1	1
sugar	1⅓ tbs.	2 tbs.	3 tbs.
salt	½ tsp.	1 tsp.	1 tsp.
yellow cornmeal	⅔ cup	1 cup	1⅓ cups
bread flour	1⅔ cups	2 cups	3 cups
yeast	1 tsp.	1½ tsp.	2½ tsp.

HONEY CORNMEAL BREAD

This is a very tasty, slightly sweet cornmeal loaf. The dough may appear wet, but it should be high-rising and light in texture as a result.

	Small	**Medium**	**Large**
water	½ cup	¾ cup	1 cup
vegetable oil	1 tbs.	1½ tbs.	2 tbs.
honey	2 tbs.	3 tbs.	¼ cup
eggs	2	3	4
salt	½ tsp.	1 tsp.	1 tsp.
cornmeal	⅔ cup	1 cup	1⅓ cups
whole wheat flour	⅓ cup	½ cup	⅔ cup
bread flour	1 cup	1½ cups	2 cups
yeast	1 tsp.	1½ tsp.	2½ tsp.

BUCKWHEAT BREAD

This is a strong tasting bread — a must for buckwheat lovers.

	Small	Medium	Large
water	1⅛ cups	1¼ cups	1½ cups
vegetable oil	1½ tbs.	2 tbs.	3 tbs.
honey	1 tbs.	1½ tbs.	2 tbs.
salt	½ tsp.	1 tsp.	1 tsp.
buckwheat flour	½ cup	⅔ cup	¾ cup
whole wheat flour	1 cup	1⅓ cups	1½ cups
bread flour	1½ cups	2 cups	2½ cups
yeast	1½ tsp.	2 tsp.	2 tsp.

THREE SEED BREAD

This bread has a wonderful taste and texture. Feel free to experiment with different seeds. Try combinations of anise, fennel, caraway or any other seeds that you have on hand.

	Small	Medium	Large
water	1 cup	1½ cups	1¾ cups
vegetable oil	1½ tbs.	2 tbs.	3 tbs.
honey	1½ tsp.	2 tsp.	1 tbs.
salt	½ tsp.	¾ tsp.	1 tsp.
sunflower seed kernels	3 tbs.	¼ cup	⅓ cup
sesame seeds	1½ tbs.	2 tbs.	3 tbs.
poppy seeds	1 tbs.	1½ tbs.	2 tbs.
whole wheat flour	1 cup	1⅓ cups	1½ cups
bread flour	2 cups	2¾ cups	3 cups
nonfat dry milk	3 tbs.	¼ cup	¼ cup
yeast	1 tsp.	2 tsp.	2½ tsp.

APPLE CHUNK BREAD

Basic cycle

This is an absolute must try. Add the apples, which add moisture to the dough, at the beginning of the second kneading cycle. Add 1 to 2 tbs. of flour to adjust the consistency if necessary (see page 12). This dessert bread should be served warm (it probably won't last long enough to get cold anyway).

	Small	**Medium**	**Large**
milk	⅔ cup	1 cup	1¼ cups
vegetable oil	2 tbs.	3 tbs.	3 tbs.
sugar	1½ tbs.	2 tbs.	2½ tbs.
cinnamon	½ tsp.	½ tsp.	1 tsp.
salt	1 tsp.	1½ tsp.	1½ tsp.
bread flour	2 cups	3 cups	3½ cups
yeast	1 tsp.	1½ tsp.	2 tsp.
medium apples, peeled and diced	½	1½	1½

APPLESAUCE BREAD

This bread was a huge hit at a neighborhood potluck — the children, especially, kept going back for more. It's a very moist loaf.

	Small	Medium	Large
applesauce	1 cup	1¼ cups	1¾ cups
margarine or butter	2 tbs.	2 tbs.	3 tbs.
sugar	1 tbs.	1½ tbs.	2 tbs.
salt	1 tsp.	1 tsp.	1½ tsp.
cinnamon, optional	1 tsp.	1 tsp.	1½ tsp.
whole wheat flour	¾ cup	1 cup	1¼ cups
bread flour	1½ cups	2 cups	2½ cups
yeast	1½ tsp.	2 tsp.	2½ tsp.

BANANA OATMEAL BREAD

This low-rising bread has a slight taste of banana with the feel of oatmeal. The flavor of the banana seems to be stronger when the bread is toasted. Use fully ripe bananas and adjust the dough consistency with the extra water if you need to (see page 12).

	Small	Medium	Large
water	⅓-½ cup	½-⅔ cup	½-¾ cup
mashed bananas	¾ cup	1 cup	1¼ cups
vegetable oil	2 tbs.	2½ tbs.	3 tbs.
sugar	1 tbs.	1½ tbs.	2 tbs.
salt	1 tsp.	1 tsp.	1½ tsp.
oats	1 cup	1⅓ cups	1¾ cups
bread flour	2 cups	2⅔ cups	3 cups
yeast	1½ tsp.	2 tsp.	2½ tsp.

STRAWBERRY BANANA BREAD

This wonderful, light loaf has just the right hint of both strawberries and bananas. Use ripe bananas and adjust the consistency with additional milk or flour if necessary (see page 12).

	Small	**Medium**	**Large**
milk	¼ cup	⅓ cup	½ cup
mashed strawberries	¼ cup	⅓ cup	½ cup
mashed bananas	¼ cup	⅓ cup	½ cup
margarine	1 tbs.	1½ tbs.	2 tbs.
sugar	1 tsp.	1½ tsp.	2 tsp.
salt	½ tsp.	¾ tsp.	1 tsp.
bread flour	2 cups	2½ cups	3½ cups
yeast	1 tsp.	1½ tsp.	2½ tsp.

BLUEBERRY BREAD

Try blue cornmeal for this delicious bread, although yellow cornmeal will do nicely too. If using frozen blueberries, they must be well thawed and tightly packed into your measuring cup. Adjust the consistency with the water as the dough is kneading (see page 12). This low-rising, dense bread is full of flavor.

	Small	**Medium**	**Large**
cottage cheese	½ cup	⅔ cup	¾ cup
margarine or butter	1½ tbs.	2 tbs.	2 tbs.
blueberries	¾ cup	1 cup	1¼ cups
sugar	2 tbs.	2½ tbs.	3 tbs.
salt	1 tsp.	1½ tsp.	1½ tsp.
blue cornmeal	1 cup	1⅓ cups	1½ cups
bread flour	2 cups	2⅔ cups	3 cups
yeast	1½ tsp.	2 tsp.	2½ tsp.
water	2-4 tbs.	3 tbs.-⅓ cup	¼-½ cup

COCONUT PINEAPPLE BREAD

This wonderful bread is a must for Sunday brunch or dessert. Or, try it for a Hawaiian Luau dinner. Adjust the consistency of the dough with the water as the dough is kneading (see page 12).

	Small	Medium	Large
cream cheese	4 oz.	6 oz.	8 oz.
crushed pineapple, drained (8 oz. can)	½ can	1 can	1 can
pineapple extract	1 tsp.	1½ tsp.	2 tsp.
vegetable oil	2 tbs.	3 tbs.	3 tbs.
sugar	2 tbs.	3 tbs.	3 tbs.
salt	¾ tsp.	1 tsp.	1 tsp.
grated coconut	3 tbs.	¼ cup	⅓ cup
bread flour	2 cups	3 cups	3½ cups
yeast	1 tsp.	1½ tsp.	2 tsp.
water	1-3 tbs.	2-4 tbs.	¼-⅓ cup

LEMON BREAD

This lightly colored bread has a subtle, pleasing flavor. The lemon peel can be adjusted to taste.

	Small	**Medium**	**Large**
water	⅔ cup	1 cup	1¼ cups
margarine or butter	1 tbs.	2 tbs.	2 tbs.
grated lemon peel	¾ tsp.	1 tsp.	1½ tsp.
sugar	½ tsp.	¾ tsp.	1 tsp.
salt	¼ tsp.	½ tsp.	¾ tsp.
bread flour	2 cups	3 cups	3½ cups
nonfat dry milk	2 tbs.	¼ cup	⅓ cup
yeast	1 tsp.	1½ tsp.	2 tsp.

ORANGE-CINNAMON BREAD

This makes delicious breakfast bread. Set it on the timer cycle and wake up to it hot from the machine, or have it toasted the next day (if it lasts that long). Both the cinnamon and the orange peel can be adjusted to taste.

	Small	Medium	Large
orange juice	¾ cup	1⅛ cups	1⅓ cups
margarine or butter	1 tbs.	2 tbs.	2 tbs.
cinnamon	1 tsp.	2 tsp.	1 tbs.
grated orange peel	¾ tsp.	1 tsp.	1 tsp.
salt	½ tsp.	¾ tsp.	1 tsp.
sugar	1 tsp.	2 tsp.	1 tbs.
bread flour	2 cups	3 cups	3½ cups
yeast	1½ tsp.	2 tsp.	2½ tsp.

RAISIN BREAD

A friend of mine tasted this bread and went out the next day to buy an automatic bread machine. Need I say more?

	Small	**Medium**	**Large**
water	¾ cup	1⅛ cups	1¼ cups
margarine or butter	1½ tbs.	2 tbs.	2 tbs.
sugar	1½ tbs.	2 tbs.	2½ tbs.
salt	¾ tsp.	1 tsp.	1 tsp.
bread flour	2 cups	3 cups	3½ cups
yeast	1 tsp.	1½ tsp.	2 tsp.
At beep add:			
raisins	½ cup	¾ cup	1 cup

VARIATIONS

All ingredients are added to the machine at the beep.

	Small	**Medium**	**Large**
CINNAMON RAISIN BREAD			
raisins	½ cup	¾ cup	1 cup
cinnamon	2 tsp.	1 tbs.	1 tbs.
ORANGE RAISIN BREAD			
raisins	½ cup	¾ cup	1 cup
grated orange peel	⅓ tsp.	½ tsp.	1 tsp.
APRICOT BREAD			
dried apricots, chopped	½ cup	¾ cup	1 cup
MIXED DRIED FRUIT BREAD			
mixed dried fruit, chopped	½ cup	¾ cup	1 cup

POTATO BREAD

This bread is really good alone or as a sandwich bread. The potatoes give it just a little extra flavor. This high-rising bread slices very well. Use an egg yolk, egg white or 2 tbs. egg substitute for the ½ egg. Boil 1 to 2 peeled potatoes and save the cooking water to use in the bread. Mash potatoes, without milk or butter, and cool to lukewarm or room temperature.

	Small	**Medium**	**Large**
potato cooking water	½ cup	⅔ cup	¾ cup
margarine or butter	2 tbs.	2½ tbs.	3 tbs.
egg	½	½	1
mashed potatoes	⅓ cup	⅓ cup	½ cup
sugar	1½ tbs.	2 tbs.	2 tbs.
salt	¾ tsp.	1 tsp.	1 tsp.
bread flour	2 cups	2½ cups	3 cups
yeast	1 tsp.	1½ tsp.	2 tsp.

SWEET POTATO BREAD

Just a hint of sweet potatoes makes this a perfect accompaniment to a turkey dinner — and it's great later for the leftover sandwiches. Cinnamon or nutmeg can be adjusted to taste if desired. Be sure to save the water used to cook the sweet potatoes for the first ingredient!

	Small	**Medium**	**Large**
sweet potato cooking water	½ cup	¾ cup	⅞ cup
mashed sweet potatoes	⅓ cup	½ cup	⅔ cup
margarine or butter	2 tbs.	3 tbs.	3 tbs.
brown sugar	2 tbs.	3 tbs.	¼ cup
salt	¾ tsp.	1 tsp.	1½ tsp.
cinnamon or nutmeg	½ tsp.	¾ tsp.	1 tsp.
bread flour	2 cups	3 cups	3½ cups
yeast	1 tsp.	1½ tsp.	2 tsp.

ONION BREAD

This is a great accompaniment to barbecue dinners, chicken or burgers. Onions vary in moisture content, so you may have to adjust the dough's consistency (see page 12).

	Small	Medium	Large
water	½ cup	¾ cup	1 cup
margarine or butter	1 tbs.	1½ tbs.	2 tbs.
grated fresh onion	⅓ cup	½ cup	⅔ cup
sugar	2 tsp.	1 tbs.	1½ tbs.
salt	¾ tsp.	1 tsp.	1½ tsp.
whole wheat flour	⅓ cup	½ cup	⅔ cup
bread flour	1¾ cups	2½ cups	3⅓ cups
yeast	1 tsp.	1½ tsp.	2½ tsp.

SALSA CORNMEAL BREAD

This wonderful cornmeal bread has just a hint of spicy salsa. Serve this low-rising bread with any Mexican meal. Adjust the consistency of the dough if necessary (see page 12).

	Small	**Medium**	**Large**
milk	⅔ cup	⅞ cup	1 cup
salsa	2 tbs.	3 tbs.	¼ cup
margarine or butter	1½ tbs.	2 tbs.	2½ tbs.
egg	1	1	1
sugar	2 tsp.	1 tbs.	1½ tbs.
salt	¾ tsp.	1 tsp.	1½ tsp.
yellow cornmeal	⅔ cup	1 cup	1⅓ cups
bread flour	2 cups	2½ cups	3 cups
yeast	1 tsp.	1½ tsp.	2 tsp.

CARROT BREAD

This delicious, healthy bread is a good way to get your beta carotene!

	Small	Medium	Large
water	¾ cup	⅞ cup	1¼ cups
vegetable oil	1 tbs.	1½ tbs.	2 tbs.
grated carrots	½ cup	⅔ cup	¾ cup
brown sugar	1½ tbs.	2 tbs.	2½ tbs.
salt	1 tsp.	1 tsp.	1½ tsp.
oats	1 cup	1⅓ cups	1½ cups
whole wheat flour	½ cup	⅔ cup	¾ cup
bread flour	1½ cups	2 cups	2½ cups
nonfat dry milk	3 tbs.	¼ cup	⅓ cup
yeast	1 tsp.	1½ tsp.	2 tsp.

ZUCCHINI WHEAT BREAD

Zucchini lovers will be especially happy with this loaf. Toasting brings out a stronger flavor. Watch the consistency of the dough and adjust with water or flour as needed (see page 12).

	Small	**Medium**	**Large**
shredded zucchini	½ cup	¾ cup	1 cup
water	½ cup	¾ cup	1 cup
vegetable oil	2 tbs.	3 tbs.	¼ cup
honey	2 tbs.	3 tbs.	¼ cup
salt	½ tsp.	¾ tsp.	1 tsp.
grated orange peel	¾ tsp.	1 tsp.	1½ tsp.
wheat germ	3 tbs.	¼ cup	⅓ cup
whole wheat flour	1 cup	1½ cups	2 cups
bread flour	1 cup	1½ cups	2 cups
yeast	1 tsp.	1½ tsp.	2 tsp.

OREGANO BREAD

This often-requested bread is an absolute must with spaghetti or lasagna. Once you have this you'll never go back to plain old garlic bread! Several bread testers have placed orders for this when entertaining with Italian meals.

	Small	**Medium**	**Large**
water	¾ cup	1⅛ cups	1½ cups
olive oil	2 tbs.	¼ cup	⅓ cup
Parmesan cheese, grated	3 tbs.	¼ cup	⅓ cup
sugar, optional	1 tsp.	1½ tsp.	2 tsp.
salt	½ tsp.	¾ tsp.	1 tsp.
dried oregano	2 tsp.	1 tbs.	1½ tbs.
bread flour	2 cups	3 cups	3½ cups
nonfat dry milk	3 tbs.	¼ cup	⅓ cup
yeast	1½ tsp.	2 tsp.	2½ tsp.

HERB BREAD

Here's a very spicy bread to perk up a meal. It's good with chicken or fish.

	Small	**Medium**	**Large**
water	⅔ cup	1⅛ cups	1¼ cups
egg	1	1	1
margarine or butter	1 tbs.	2 tbs.	2½ tbs.
salt	¼ tsp.	½ tsp.	1 tsp.
sugar	1 tbs.	1½ tbs.	2 tbs.
dried oregano	¼ tsp.	½ tsp.	1 tsp.
dried thyme	¼ tsp.	½ tsp.	1 tsp.
black pepper	¼ tsp.	½ tsp.	1 tsp.
dried parsley	¼ tsp.	½ tsp.	1 tsp.
celery seeds	dash	⅛ tsp.	¼ tsp.
dried sage	dash	⅛ tsp.	¼ tsp.
wheat germ	3 tbs.	¼ cup	⅓ cup
oats	3 tbs.	¼ cup	⅓ cup
bread flour	2 cups	3 cups	3½ cups
yeast	1½ tsp.	2 tsp.	2½ tsp.

PARSLEY HERB BREAD

*This is another good bread to serve with chicken. It's not as spicy as the **Herb Bread**, page 67, but it adds a nice flavor to the meal.*

	Small	**Medium**	**Large**
water	¾ cup	1 cup	1¼ cups
olive oil	1 tbs.	1½ tbs.	2 tbs.
sugar	1 tsp.	1½ tsp.	2 tsp.
salt	½ tsp.	1 tsp.	1 tsp.
dried parsley	1½ tsp.	2 tsp.	1 tbs.
dried chives	¼ tsp.	½ tsp.	1 tsp.
dried tarragon	¼ tsp.	½ tsp.	1 tsp.
bread flour	2 cups	3 cups	3½ cups
yeast	1 tsp.	1½ tsp.	2 tsp.

DILL BREAD

This outstanding bread is great with either pasta or fish. It's one of our favorites, and another often-requested bread. The amount of cottage cheese is the same for all sizes; the eggs provide additional moisture. Expect a high-rising loaf.

	Small	**Medium**	**Large**
cottage cheese	1 cup	1 cup	1 cup
eggs	1	2	3
sugar	1½ tbs.	2 tbs.	3 tbs.
dill weed	2 tsp.	1 tbs.	1½ tbs.
salt	½ tsp.	½ tsp.	1 tsp.
baking soda	¼ tsp.	¼ tsp.	½ tsp.
bread flour	2 cups	2½ cups	3 cups
yeast	1 tsp.	1½ tsp.	2 tsp.

GARLIC PARMESAN BREAD

If you're a garlic bread lover, this is for you. Feel free to increase or decrease the amount of garlic powder to suit your taste. This loaf is very aromatic and is, of course, great with Italian meals. Make sure the garlic powder is fresh (it gets bitter if it sits on your shelf too long), and use freshly grated Parmesan cheese.

	Small	**Medium**	**Large**
water	⅔ cup	1 cup	1⅛ cups
margarine or butter	2 tbs.	2½ tbs.	3 tbs.
honey	2 tsp.	1 tbs.	1½ tbs.
Parmesan cheese, grated	½ cup	⅔ cup	¾ cup
salt	½ tsp.	¾ tsp.	1 tsp.
garlic powder	1 tsp.	1½ tsp.	2 tsp.
bread flour	2 cups	3 cups	3½ cups
yeast	1 tsp.	1½ tsp.	2 tsp.

CHRISTMAS ANISE BREAD

Anise seeds add nice flavor to this bread but it's not overwhelming. If you want a stronger-tasting bread, you can safely double the amount of anise and other spices.

	Small	Medium	Large
milk	⅔ cup	1 cup	1¼ cups
margarine or butter	2 tbs.	2½ tbs.	3 tbs.
sugar	1 tbs.	1½ tbs.	2 tbs.
salt	½ tsp.	¾ tsp.	1 tsp.
anise seeds	1 tsp.	1½ tsp.	2 tsp.
mace	dash	⅛ tsp.	¼ tsp.
nutmeg	dash	⅛ tsp.	¼ tsp.
grated lemon peel	½ tsp.	¾ tsp.	1 tsp.
grated orange peel	½ tsp.	¾ tsp.	1 tsp.
bread flour	2 cups	3 cups	3½ cups
yeast	1½ tsp.	2 tsp.	2½ tsp.

COFFEE SPICE BREAD

This is similar in taste to a brown bread and is a great way to use up that left-over coffee — regular or decaf!

	Small	**Medium**	**Large**
brewed coffee	½ cup	¾ cup	1 cup
vegetable oil	2 tbs.	2½ tbs.	3 tbs.
egg	1	1	1
sugar	2 tbs.	3 tbs.	¼ cup
salt	¾ tsp.	1 tsp.	1 tsp.
cinnamon	¾ tsp.	1 tsp.	1 tsp.
ground cloves	⅛ tsp.	¼ tsp.	½ tsp.
allspice	⅛ tsp.	¼ tsp.	½ tsp.
bread flour	2 cups	3 cups	3½ cups
yeast	1 tsp.	1½ tsp.	2 tsp.

CROISSANT LOAF

This delicious loaf has flaky layers similar to croissants.

½ cup water
2 tbs. margarine or butter
1 tsp. vanilla extract
2 eggs
¼ cup sugar

¾ tsp. salt
3 cups all-purpose flour
2 tsp. yeast
3 tbs. butter or margarine, cut into
    small pieces

Place water, margarine, vanilla, eggs, sugar, salt, flour and yeast in the bread machine pan in the order listed. Make dough on the dough cycle.

When dough cycle is complete, remove dough from pan and roll into a ½-inch-thick rectangle. Place ½ of the remaining butter on the middle third of dough. Fold one third over onto top of butter. Place remaining butter pieces on top of folded-over third and fold remaining third over butter. Roll dough into another rectangle and fold into thirds, as you would a business letter. Wrap dough loosely in waxed paper and refrigerate for about 20 minutes. Roll dough into a rectangle and fold into thirds 3 more times. Chill dough in the refrigerator if it seems sticky and difficult to work with. Lightly knead dough, shaping into a ball. Place dough in a greased loaf pan. Cover and let rise for 50 to 60 minutes or until doubled in bulk. Bake in a preheated 350° oven for 30 to 35 minutes or until golden brown. Makes 1 loaf.

ALMOND BUTTER CRESCENTS

These croissant-style rolls are extremely simple to make.

DOUGH
½ cup milk
¼ cup butter
1½ tsp. almond extract
2 eggs
⅓ cup sugar
½ tsp. salt
3-3¼ cups all-purpose flour
1½ tsp. yeast

FILLING
2 tbs. melted butter
1 tsp. almond extract

GLAZE
1 egg beaten with 1 tbs. water

For dough, place milk, butter, almond extract, eggs, sugar, salt, flour and yeast in the bread machine pan in the order listed. Make dough on the dough cycle.

When dough cycle is complete, remove dough form machine and roll into a large circle on a lightly floured surface. Mix filling ingredients and brush over dough. Cut circle into 8 wedges, as you would a pie. Roll each piece from wide end to tip of triangle and curve slightly to form a crescent. Brush each crescent with glaze. Place crescents on a cornmeal-covered baking sheet, cover and let rise for about 1 hour. Bake in a preheated 350° oven for 15 to 20 minutes, or until golden brown. Makes 8.

VARIATION: ALMOND NUT CRESCENTS
Sprinkle about ¼ cup chopped almonds on top of filling before cutting into wedges.

CINNAMON ROLLS

These rolls are very good and not overly sweet. If you want a sweeter roll, make a glaze out of milk and powdered sugar to spread over the tops while still warm. Baking these rolls in muffin cups makes them rise beautifully and look uniform.

1 cup milk
2 tbs. butter
1 egg
2 tbs. sugar
½ tsp. salt
3-3½ cups all-purpose flour

1½ tsp. yeast
2 tbs. butter, melted, or more if desired
1½ tbs. cinnamon
¼ cup sugar
½ cup raisins, optional

Place milk, butter, egg, sugar, salt, flour and yeast in the bread machine pan in the order listed. Make dough on the dough cycle.

Remove dough from machine. Roll dough into a rectangle and brush with melted butter. Mix cinnamon with sugar and sprinkle over dough. Top with raisins, if using. Roll up dough jelly roll-style and cut into 1½-inch-wide slices. Place each slice in a muffin cup, cover and let rise for 35 to 40 minutes. Brush tops lightly with melted butter, if desired. Bake in a preheated 400° oven for 20 to 25 minutes, until golden brown. Makes 12.

SWEET ROLLS

These special treats are wonderful topped with jam.

¾ cup milk
¼ cup margarine or butter
1 egg
¼ cup sugar
1 tsp. salt
3 cups all-purpose flour
2 tsp. yeast

Place milk, margarine, egg, sugar, salt, flour and yeast in the bread machine pan in the order listed. Make dough on the dough cycle.

Remove dough from machine. Shape dough into 12 balls and place in muffin cups. Cover and let rise for 45 to 60 minutes. Bake in a preheated 350° oven for 15 to 20 minutes, or until golden brown. Makes 12.

PARKER HOUSE DINNER ROLLS

Now synonymous with American dinner rolls, these originated at The Parker House in Boston.

1 cup milk
2 tbs. margarine or butter
1 egg
1 tbs. sugar
½ tsp. salt
2½-3 cups all-purpose flour
2 tsp. yeast
3-4 tbs. butter, melted
1 egg, beaten

Place milk, margarine, egg, sugar, salt, flour and yeast in the bread machine pan in the order listed. Make dough on the dough cycle.

Remove dough from machine. Knead dough by hand for about 5 minutes. With a rolling pin, roll out dough and cut into 12 rounds with a biscuit cutter or cup. Brush rounds with melted butter. Fold rounds in half and place in buttered muffin tins. Cover and let rise for 35 to 45 minutes. Brush tops with beaten egg and bake in a preheated 350° oven for 20 to 25 minutes, until golden brown. Makes 12.

HAMBURGER OR HOT DOG ROLLS

Make plenty of these and freeze the extras for the next time — if you have any left, that is! They're wonderful as is, but you can also add flavorings. Add 1½ tbs. of one of the following to the dough: sesame seeds, poppy seeds, chives or minced onion. You can also brush the tops of the buns with a beaten egg and sprinkle with sesame seeds immediately prior to baking.

1 cup water
2 tbs. margarine or butter
2 tbs. sugar
2 tsp. salt
3-3¼ cups bread flour
3 tbs. nonfat dry milk
2 tsp. yeast

Place water, margarine, sugar, salt, flour, dry milk and yeast in the bread machine pan in the order listed. Make dough on the dough cycle.

Remove dough from machine. Punch down dough and let rest for 20 minutes. Form dough into 12 balls. Shape dough into desired bun shapes and flatten slightly. Cover and let rise for 1 hour. Place buns on a lightly greased baking sheet and bake in a preheated 375° oven for 15 to 20 minutes, or until golden brown. Makes 12.

SANDWICH ROLLS

These are wonderful hot out of the oven, whether you make sandwiches with them or not.

1¼ cups water
2 tbs. vegetable oil
2 tsp. sugar
1 tsp. salt
3-3¼ cups bread flour
⅓ cup nonfat dry milk or buttermilk powder
1½ tsp. yeast

Place water, oil, sugar, salt, flour, dry milk and yeast in the bread machine pan in the order listed. Make dough on the dough cycle.

Remove dough from machine. Form dough into 10 or 12 balls, shape balls into rolls and let rise for 40 to 50 minutes on a lightly greased baking sheet. Bake in a preheated 375° oven for 20 minutes or until golden brown. Makes 10 to 12.

WHOLE WHEAT SANDWICH ROLLS

These are wonderfully tasty, as well as nutritious. To vary this recipe, use flavored olive oil or walnut oil in place of the vegetable oil.

1⅛ cups water
2 tbs. vegetable oil
1 tbs. honey
1½ tsp. salt
1 cup whole wheat flour
2 tbs. wheat or oat bran
¼ cup wheat germ
2 cups bread flour
1½ tsp. yeast

Place water, oil, honey, salt, wheat flour, bran, wheat germ, bread flour and yeast in the bread machine pan in the order listed. Make dough on the dough cycle.

Remove dough from machine. Form dough into 12 balls. Shape balls into rolls and let rise for 50 to 60 minutes on a lightly greased baking sheet. Bake in a preheated 375° oven for 20 minutes or until golden brown. Makes 12.

CHALLAH

Challah is a very light and wonderful-tasting bread. The dough is somewhat moist, and you should add only enough flour to prevent sticking, either while the machine is kneading or after the dough has been removed.

⅔ cup water
2 eggs
2 tbs. vegetable oil
2 tbs. sugar
1 tsp. salt
3-3¼ cups bread flour
1½ tsp. yeast
1 egg, beaten
poppy seeds, optional

Place water, eggs, oil, sugar, salt, flour and yeast in the bread machine pan in the order listed. Make dough on the dough cycle.

Remove dough from machine and divide into 3 pieces; roll each piece into a rope about 14 inches long and braid on a greased baking sheet. Cover and let rise for about 45 minutes. Brush top with egg and sprinkle with poppy seeds, if desired. Bake in a preheated 350° oven for 45 minutes. Makes 1 loaf.

LITHUANIAN COFFEE BREAD

Tom and Rasa, friends of Lithuanian descent, said this tasted just like the coffee breads their mothers used to make.

½ cup milk
¼ cup margarine or butter
2 eggs
1 tsp. vanilla extract
½ tsp. salt
½ cup sugar
1 tsp. grated lemon peel

3-3¼ cups bread flour
1½ tsp. yeast
¼ cup sugar
¼ cup chopped walnuts
½ cup raisins
1 egg, beaten

Place milk, margarine, eggs, vanilla, salt, sugar, lemon peel, flour and yeast in the bread machine pan in the order listed. Make dough on the dough cycle.

Remove dough from machine and shape into 3 long, thin rectangles. Mix sugar, walnuts and raisins. Spread ⅓ of the walnut-raisin mixture along the middle of each rectangle and fold dough over filling to encase it. Braid rectangles together and place in a lightly greased loaf pan. Let rise for about 30 minutes. Brush with beaten egg. Bake in a preheated 350° oven for 30 to 35 minutes until brown. Makes 1 loaf.

PITA BREAD

This is a definite must-try. It's well worth the few minutes involved to make it. It's easy to have done in time for lunch sandwiches.

1⅓ cups water
3 tbs. olive oil
1½ tbs. sugar
1 tsp. salt
2 cups bread flour
1½ cups whole wheat flour
2 tsp. yeast

Place water, oil, sugar, salt, flours and yeast in the bread machine pan in the order listed. Make dough on the dough cycle.

Remove dough from machine and divide into 10 balls. Flatten each ball into a disk, rolling each one into a circle of about 6 inches. Place on a baking sheet, let rise for about 20 minutes and bake in a preheated 500° oven for 8 to 10 minutes. Makes 10.

BREADSTICKS

These are far better than the ones you buy in the store. Bake enough to kee on hand. Each of the different toppings changes the flavor of the sticks — try them all. The shorter the baking time, the softer they are; the longer the baking time, the crunchier.

1⅓ cups water
1 tbs. margarine or butter
1½ tbs. sugar
1½ tsp. salt
4 cups bread flour

2 tsp. yeast
1 egg white mixed with 1 tbs. water
toppings: coarse salt, sesame seeds,
    poppy seeds, anise seeds or dried
    onion bits

Place water, margarine, sugar, salt, flour and yeast in the bread machine pan in the order listed. Make dough on the dough cycle.

Remove dough from machine and cut into small egg-sized pieces; roll pieces into ropes and place on a greased baking sheet. Cover and let rise for 20 minutes. Brush sticks with egg mixture and sprinkle with desired toppings. Bake in a preheated 400° oven for 15 minutes, or until golden brown. Makes about 24.

CRUSTY PIZZA DOUGH

If you make pizza dough once in your bread machine, you will probably never buy commercial pizza again!

	Small (one 14-inch pizza)	**Medium** (one 16-inch pizza)	**Large** (two 14-inch pizzas)
water	⅔ cup	1 cup	1⅓ cups
olive oil	1 tbs.	1½ tbs.	2 tbs.
salt	½ tsp.	½ tsp.	¾ tsp.
all-purpose flour	1 cup	1½ cups	2 cups
whole wheat flour	1 cup	1½ cups	2 cups
yeast	1 tsp.	1½ tsp.	2 tsp.
olive oil	as needed	as needed	as needed

Place water, oil, salt, flours and yeast in the bread machine pan in the order listed. Make dough on the dough cycle.

Remove dough from machine and roll into a rectangle or circle. Place on a baking sheet and turn excess under, forming a crust on the edges. Brush very lightly with olive oil. For a thick, chewy crust, cover and let rise for about 30 minutes. Top with pizza sauce, cheese and other desired toppings. Bake in a preheated 500° oven for 5 to 10 minutes, or until crust is brown and cheese is melted.

CHEESY PIZZA DOUGH

The cheese gives this pizza crust an interesting taste and texture.

	Small (one 14-inch pizza)	**Medium** (one 16-inch pizza)	**Large** (two 14-inch pizzas)
water	⅔ cup	1 cup	1⅓ cups
olive oil	2 tsp.	1 tbs.	1⅓ tbs.
shredded mozzarella	⅓ cup	½ cup	⅔ cup
salt	½ tsp.	½ tsp.	¾ tsp.
all-purpose flour	1 cup	1½ cups	2 cups
whole wheat flour	1 cup	1½ cups	2 cups
yeast	1 tsp.	1½ tsp.	2½ tsp.
olive oil	as needed	as needed	as needed

Place water, oil, cheese, salt, flours and yeast in the bread machine pan in the order listed. Make dough on the dough cycle.

Remove dough from machine and roll into a rectangle or circle. Place on a baking pan and turn excess under, forming a crust on the edges. Brush very lightly with olive oil. For a thick, chewy crust, cover and let rise for about 30 minutes. Top with pizza sauce, cheese and other desired toppings. Bake in a preheated 500° oven for 5 to 10 minutes, or until crust is brown and cheese is melted.

BAGELS

In frustration, I was led to a local bagel bakery where they shared some bagel-making hints with me. Here is the successful result.

1 cup water
1½ tbs. honey
1 tsp. salt
1 cup whole wheat flour

2 cups bread flour
1½ tsp. yeast
toppings: sesame seeds, poppy seeds,
    anise seeds or dried onion bits

Place water, honey, salt, flours and yeast in the bread machine pan in the order listed. Make dough on the dough cycle, letting the machine knead the dough once. Stop machine and let dough rise for 20 minutes.

Remove dough from machine and divide into 12 pieces. Roll each piece into a short rope and form a circle, pressing ends together. You may find it necessary to wet one end slightly to help seal ends together. Place bagels on a well-greased baking sheet, cover and let rise for only 15 to 20 minutes. Meanwhile, bring about 2 inches of water to a slight boil in a nonaluminum pan (I use a cast iron skillet). Carefully lower 3 or 4 bagels at a time into water, cooking for about 30 seconds on each side. Remove bagels, drain on a towel and sprinkle with topping, if desired. Return to greased baking sheet and bake in a preheated 550° oven for 8 minutes. Makes 12.

PRETZELS

I bet you can't eat just one!

1⅓ cups water
2 tbs. margarine or butter
1½ tbs. sugar
¾ tsp. salt
4 cups all-purpose flour

2½ tsp. yeast
4 cups water
1½ tbs. baking soda
coarse or Kosher salt

Place water, margarine, sugar, salt, flour and yeast in the bread machine pan in the order listed. Make dough on the dough cycle.

Remove dough from machine and cut into short strips. Roll strips into ropes, shape into pretzels and place on a greased baking sheet. Cover and let rise for about 45 minutes. In a cast iron or other nonaluminum skillet, bring water and baking soda almost to a boil. By hand or slotted spoon, gently lower pretzels into water for about 1 minute, turning once. Do not let water come to a full boil. Remove pretzels and return to greased baking sheet. Sprinkle with salt. Bake in a preheated 475° oven for about 12 minutes. Makes 15 to 24, depending on size.

INDEX